Loretta Santini

CITIES OF ITALY

MANTUA

GUIDE WITH CITY MAP

Sole Distributor

OREMPULLER
Fotoedizioni - Trento
www.orempuller.com

Published and printed by

NARNI - TERNI

INTRODUCTION

From any side the tourist comes, to reach Mantua he will have to pass through a long stretch of land, namely the Plain of the Po. After so many kilometres, his eyes are used to that unchanging landscape, to that space which seems infinite and indefinite. The Plain of the Po discloses itself slowly with its cultivations, rows of plants, neat country-houses, which are isolated but, at the same time, connected to other social centres by a network of roads, paths and canals. Here and there appears a village or a larger group of houses. Agricultural centres, farms, all bear witness to the need and determination to connect, even more strictly, economic activities to the social life of this large area.

When one has become accustomed to such unchanging images, which look evanescent through the fog, the town itself, which suddenly appears on the

scene, looks like a mirage. It is thus that Mantua presents itself: it emerges from the plain like an image of our mind. And it is even more so when a light fog, shading off its outline, blends it with the rest of nature, and makes it appear hanging in the air, at the borders between reality and fable. (Here we must say that fog is a very common phenomenon in this area, and very unpleasant, too, especially when it becomes so thick that visibility is very poor).

Such an impression does not change, when one realizes that Mantua looks as though it is hanging on the water, lazily lying on an island. As a matter of fact, a sea or a large river makes the town stand out of the rest of the landscape, and live in its own world. But now we should look better and more objectively at the geographical situation of Mantua, which makes it so peculiar and fascinating.

THE GEOGRAPHICAL SITUATION

Mantua occupies the south-east point of Lombardy, lying on the stretch of the Plain of the Po, where the river Mincio meets the Po. And it is the river Mincio, which, flowing quietly and solemnly, surrounds the town. This river, having come out of the lake of Garda, flows towards East, slowing down and forming very large loops.

Once it formed some marshes flowing into the plain. Through the centuries and because of silts, it formed some islets, on which Mantua rose like a lacunar town, like a new Venice.

Even today Mantua goes on living on these islets, surrounded, as we have said, by the Mincio on three sides at least (but once the river surrounded it completely).

This stretch of the river is here called Upper, Middle and Lower Lake, separated one from the other by the Mills Bridge and St. George's Bridge, such is the geographic situation which makes this town so peculiar and unique.

In fact, its position and aspect are exalted; its history and beauty are protected as by a natural coffer; its very atmosphere is full of memories and suggestions; the colours themselves are imbued with the patina of time and shade off continually because of the reflection of the water and that chromatic blend which so frequently takes place between the sky and the plain (as between the sky and the water) in particular conditions of light and atmosphere.

MANTUA AND ITS HISTORY

Mantua is a very ancient town and consequently its origins are legendary and not very clearly definable.

Probably there were groups of prehistoric people who settled on the islets the Mincio had formed with its silts.

The surrounding plain must have favoured their agricultural and pastoral economy, while the marshes were for them a sort of stronghold or safety belt. Their houses were probably pile-buildings, quite widespread in all that area, because they were fit for that particular environment. In his Aeneid, Virgil tells us of Mantua in legendary terms, since what he presents as history certainly has little to do with reality.

According to the poet, the town was founded by the Etruscans, by order of the mythical hero Ocnus, while the name derived from Mantus (an Etruscan deity). As a matter of fact, Virgil makes a muddle of the latter name and no record proves that it was of Etruscan origin.

What we know is that these people spread towards North around the 7th-6th century B. C. , occupying the Plain of the Po more towards west than towards east, where the Venetian population particularly opposed their penetration.

If Mantua was founded by the Estruscans, it must have been more a centre for their traffic than a true settlement.

It is certain that the Gauls settled in Mantua for a short time, and then it was ruled by the Romans. We know of this historical period, when this area passed under the Romans, since it is Virgil himself who, in his Bucolics complains about the expropriation of lands ordered in this area by the emperor Octavian in favour of his soldiers.

The town was linked to the destiny of Rome, keeping a mainly agricultural economy, as when later it suffered from the various invasions (Goths, Longobards, Franks), which took place after the decline of the Roman Empire.

The town underwent feudal organization (it was part of the estate of Countess Mathilda of Canossa) and later became a free town.

During the latter period it enjoyed independence and freedom, while the citizens took part in the political and social life and the economic situation flourished.

Many works were projected and completed to embellish the town and others were planned in order to regulate the course of the Mincio, which formed a large marsh around it.

In the second half of the 13th century Mantua passed under the rule of Pinamonte Bonacolsi. Many works were executed by his order, among which it is enough to mention the group of houses, which later would form the privitive core of the Ducal Palace. His power lasted till 1328, when the long and significant rule of the Gonzaga family began.

It was under this noble family that the town knew periods of great artistic, cultural and economic splendour.

Its fame and political importance went beyond the area ruled by the Gonzaga, and influenced Lombardy and the rest of Italy. Therefore, Mantua has been rightly called «the town of the Gonzaga», a name which it still keeps, mainly thanks to the numerous and important works which embellish it and bear witness to that active cultural period including four centuries of history, from the 14th century to the 18th century.

It was at that time that Mantua was shaped as it mostly remains today.

The primitive medieval core was transformed and the whole town was restructured according to the prevailing Renaissance taste.

Renowned writers, architects and painters worked in Mantua during this period. The cultural role of the town was very important, if we consider that artists such as Pisanello, Brunelleschi, Alberti, Mantegna and Giulio Romano honoured it with their art. And we must say that the Gonzaga were those who, with their Maecenatism and political determination fostered all these transformations.

Think of Ludovico II, who was surrounded by the most famous artists of that time, and impressed on the town and the court the mark of the Renaissance taste, with a Tuscan touch.

Having come to power in 1444, he followed a very wise policy, always ready to have contacts with other rulers, mainly with the Estense and Medici families. This policy was useful not only in political life, but also in terms of cultural and literary exchanges.

Under Ludovico II, Mantua became a very important town. In 1459 a diet took place here, convoked by pope Pius II, in order to organize a crusade against the Turks.

This fact bears witness to the importance of Mantua during

this period of time.

After the brief rule of Federico Gonzaga, the young Francesco ruled the town, helped by his wife Isabella of Este.

Under her, educated at the court of Ferrara, Mantua went through another significant period from the cultural and artistic point of view and lived the time of the Renaissance very intensely.

Federico II, Isabella's son, who came to power in 1519, fostered a new phase of the artistic history of the town.

It was under him that Giulio Romano worked. He projected and realized large architectonic works, which were to give a new look to the town, influencing also the following works of other artists.

The court of the Gonzaga and Mantua with it knew other periods of splendour under Gugliel-mo and then under Vincenzo I.

We are now at the beginning of the 17th century. From that time on the political and economic decline of Mantua began.

We must add to all this the despoliation of most of the pictorial works adorning the houses and churches.

The Gonzaga ruled the town till 1707, but they lost most of their political importance. And it was in 1707 that Mantua lost its political independence, passing under Austrian domination.

But, having lost its autonomy, the town did not lose its creative fervour.

As a matter of fact, cultural activity, patronized by the Augsburg Empire itself, went on with profit.

This domination was briefly interrupted when Napoleon annexed the town to the Cisalpine Republic. The Congress of Vienna, however, allotted it again to the Austrian Empire.

Since that time, the history of Mantua is like that of so many Italian towns and regions, which faced the hard and long struggles of the "Risorgimento".

But such struggles were even harder for Mantua, because it was one of the strongholds of the famous Quadrilateral.

Lastly, Mantua, too, was annexed to the Kingdom of Italy, and its history blent with the national one.

AN OUTLINE OF ITS CULTURAL AND ARTISTIC HISTORY

When outlining the cultural and artistic phenomena which have characterized this town, one should always take into account some essential facts, and most of all the whole geographical area, into which Mantua is inserted.

Consequently, when speaking of artistic currents such as the Romanesque and Gothic styles (phenomena quite widespread in Italy), we should speak rather of Romanesque- Lombard and Gothic-Lombard styles, which are phenomena including local tendencies and particular elements.

Then one must refer to the historical period and particularly to the presence of the Gonzaga, because it was under them that the premises necessary to the enlargement and embellishment of the town were created.

Lastly, considering the great number of artists who worked in Mantua, one should take into account those who were the key-artists, that is those around whom the main tendencies revolved, and those who left a more lasting mark of their art.

Before the Middle Ages, we do not have examples and testimonies of the artistic history of Mantua.

There are neither Etruscan remains (after all we are not sure about their presence in the area) nor Roman remains.

The artistic vitality, though, of the medieval period is well documented with its developments, by the structure of some areas of Mantua and some buildings.

The ancient Herbs, Broletto and Sordello Squares with the buildings surrounding them, the towers, the houses and the porticoes are medieval. Among others, we should mention the Bonacolsi palaces, the Palace of Reason and the Mayor's Palace, the Rotunda of St. Laurence and various churches in the town. The Romanesque style still persists together with the Gothic syle in many other churches or in part of them, even though successive modifications and restorations have often altered their aspects.

In the painting field, we find very interesting examples among the paintings of Tommaso of Modena and Stefano of Verona, Pisanello, recently rediscovered, and many other artists, who remained unknown, like those who painted the series of the "warriors" in the Ducal Palace.

The humanistic-Renaissance phenomenon was much longer and complex, and mainly it was more open to outside influences. Under the Gonzaga family, first of all the town changed its urban structure.

At the same time, great transformation and decoration works went on in the ancient palaces.

The magnificent Ducal Palace was enriched with many masterpieces, while various parts were completely restructured.

Leon Battista Alberti worked in Mantua in the churches of St. Andrew and St. Sebastian, reproposing a new classical syntax and consequently the values of antiquity.

At the same time Luca Fancelli also worked there, an artist who tried to meet the needs of Duke Ludovico II, who, wishing to put order into the town-planning, looked at the canons of the humanistic-Renaissance art, which had asserted itself in Tuscany.

In the painting field it was Andrea Mantegna that created, in the second half of the 15th century, the masterpiece of the "Room of the Married Couple". Renaissance art reached its height and Mantua enjoyed a productive and very happy period, which placed it among the towns of art.

During the 16th century, all the previous tendencies developed and the artistic history of Mantua becomes more complex. Writers and thinkers formed true cultural circles in the courts.

According to the wishes of Isabella of Este many renowned artists settled in Mantua and her rooms were enriched with the masterpieces of the most famous painters of her times, becoming thus true art-galleries.

It was, however, Duke Federico II that invited Giulio Romano to the town. It was the beginning of the 16th century. For some years Mantua watched his unceasing activity and the look of the town was completely changed.

He built the Tea Palace, his own house the Rustica, the

"Pescerie", the Cathedral, the Citadel Gate et cetera. Giulio Romano, in all these works, developing and re-presenting a substantial classical language, charged it with new effects, often powerful and scenographic, thus bearing witness to the anxieties and dissatisfactions of the first artists working in the late-Renaissance period, since it was impossible to re-create a serene and perfect world.

Giulio Romano, who was also a painter, himself worked on, or designed for his pupils, the decoration of the interiors of these buildings, leaving thus a great number of works, which influenced the taste of the time and other artists as well, for a long time.

Among the other architects who worked in Mantua during the same period, we should not forget Bertani (who worked on the Church of St. Barbara, the Exhibition Courtyard, experimenting in them, as in other buildings, new architectonic techniques); Viani, who worked in the church of St. Ursula and St. Mauritius, in some halls of the Ducal Palace, in the Palace of the Gonzaga of Vescovato, and was present, also in terms of paintings, in various places.

In the painting field, apart from the above mentioned Giulio Romano, many artists worked to fresco the rooms of the various palaces or the chapels of the churches.

They were Lorenzo Costa the Younger, Domenico Fetti, Bedoli and many others who painted after the models of the late-Renaissance style, full of "chiaroscuro", new effects, and sensations, and new tendencies anticipating the Baroque style.

During the 17th century some Baroque buildings were constructed, such as the above mentioned Palace of the Gonzaga of Vescovato by Viani or the Sordi Palace, with their respective decorations.

During the 18th century more works were realized than in the past. The churches of St. Barbara, the Theatre, the Palace of the Academy were built; the large Virgilian Square was re-arranged.

Various artists worked, such as Bibiena, Piermarini, Dal Pozzo, who used the predominant neo-classical forms, though showing their personal taste in some of their works.

The artistic itinerary we have outlined here, though it does not investigate all the aspects of the subject, is certainly useful to follow more closely, during a visit to the town, the various stages, through which Mantua developed, and to put into perspective, in a more logical and orderly way, the various phases of this transformation.

AN OUTLINE OF ITS ECONOMIC ACTIVITY

Mantua, the main town of the south-east point of Lombardy, lies, with all its territory, in the low valley of the Po and is an integral part of it also from the economic point of view. Its economy is flourishing especially in the agricultural field.

The very presence of the plain has brought it to an increasing development of cultivations organized according to more modern and rational criteria.

Forage, wheat, corn, but also rice, vines, sugar beet, are all sure sources of income. However, through the patient work of hundreds of years, it has been necessary to regulate the courses of the rivers.

In fact, their waters flowed and remained on impermeable grounds and, having formed large marshes, hindered any activity. This is the reason why the reclamation works began with the life itself of the town, improving through the centuries till they rendered the whole area stable and logistically well organized. Industry, too, has developed gradually and now includes various sectors.

Trade is flourishing, thanks also to a very efficient road and railway network.

In short, the economy of this province is active and modern and has become very important, in the whole Lombard area and, more generally, in the Po area.

Mantua, as all the towns which have a long and intense historical and cultural life, has a very interesting architectonic cenue consisting mainly of the Herbs, Broletto, Mantegna and Sordello squares. These ones and the buildings surrounding them, represented and still represent the key-points of Mantua's political, religious and cultural activities. Apart from this central area, other monuments, quite important from the historical and artistic points of view, embellish the town. It is much better, however, to visit it beginning from the place, which historically has represented the ideal centre of Mantua's life.

Herbs Square

is part and parcel of this centre and it is very interesting thanks to the various buildings surrounding it.

It is mainly rectangular and characterized by a long series of porticoes, under which there are many shops.

The brown-reddish colour of the bricks (with which the long Palace of Reason is built) prevails, together with that of the brown-amber coloured houses closing it on the other sides. Apart from the Palace of Reason, the Mayor's Palace, the Clock Tower, the Rotunda of St. Laurence and merchant Boniforte's house surround the Herbs Square (so called because of the characteristic market which traditionally takes place here).

The Mayor's Palace

The Mayor's Palace closes the square on one of its shorter sides and faces it with its back façade, while the main front faces the near-by Broletto Square. The original structure of the palace is medieval and, as an epigraph tells us, it was built in 1227.

As the name itself shows, the

palace was the seat of the town government.

Later on the building was transformed (mainly in the facade) and restored by Luca Fancelli, the artist through whom Duke Ludovico Gonzaga wanted to give a concrete shape to humanistic-Renaissance art which had spread all over Tuscany.

As it is now, we can distinguish, in this building, two creative stages and must admit that the rough but powerful simplicity of the original architecture has been partially altered by successive transformations. Notice on the facade the statue representing "Virgil on a throne" (it is placed in a niche surmounted by an ogival arch).

The Palace of Reason

closes the Herbs Square on the east side.

It is an embattled building, imposing and, at the same time, quite agile. It was built in 1250.

Along the body of the building there is a series of arches including mullioned windows with three lights, underlined by

---

The Herbs Square

small marble columns.

The optic and chromatic effect is very good, thanks to the play of light and shade created by these arches, in constrast with the white colour of the small columns set into the reddish surface of the bricks.

On the lower part opens, below a penthouse, a portico, built in the 16th century, but restored much later, and therefore not in harmony with the rest of the architecture.

The Palace of Reason was a seat of the High Court of Justice, a justice which was administered in the very large hall, which you can visit on the 1st Floor.

In this austere hall we can still admire parts of the frescoes which once adorned it and constitute one of the few testimonies of the medieval pictorial art in Mantua.

They consist of a cycle of "warriors" (12th century) and another of religious figures (made in the 13th century by a certain Crisopolo), which have been inspired by Byzantine-like models, which are very far from the predominant Romanesque painting quite widespread in this geographic area.

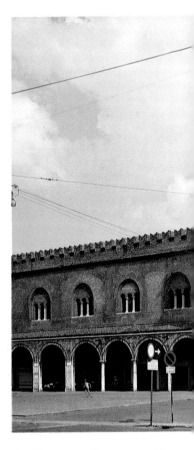

the Madonna placed in a niche of the Tower itself, dates back to the 17th century.

❦

The Clock Tower

adjoins the preceding Palace of Reason, facing the square with its big structure and warm colour of the bricks.

Its name comes from the clock set into it, which in the past constituted a quite complex and ingenious piece of machinery.

The tower was built by the above mentioned Luca Fancelli, who built it according to the classical models followed in most parts of Italy. The statue of

The Rotunda of St. Laurence

closes the east side of the square together with the above mentioned palace of Reason and Clock Tower.

The building is today a little below the level of the Herbs Square.

It is a beautiful church in Romanesque style, built towards the end of the 11th century.

It is a simple and atmospheric round building made of bricks.

The Palace of Reason.

The outside surface of the church is divided by slender pilaster strips crowned on top by a series of small hanging arches: these motifs characterize Romanesque architecture to a large extent.

Above, the dome apears hidden by a cylindrical structure, smaller than the lower one.

It is also crowned by a series of small pensile arches, which slightly underline the wall with a light "chiaroscuro".

Above it, a conic penthouse covers the building.

The interior of the Rotunda of St. Laurence is simple and, at the same time, evocative thanks to its simple structures and bare walls.

The interior, too, is round, with brick columns all around, supporting the vaults.

A certain agility is given to this architecture by the second circle of columns on the upper floor, creating other chiaroscuro effects.

The Rotunda of St. Laurence was built by order of Countess Mathilda of Canossa.

The large staircase of the Palace of Reason.

Mercante Boniforte's House

In the same Herbs Square we can still admire the Gothic-like architecture of the merchant Boniforte's HOUSE.

As a matter of fact, it was built in various styles, bearing witness to the tendency of the 15th century bourgeoisie to draw attention to themselves with an ostentatious outward show of wealth, thus making their economic standing felt and seen. We must admit, however, that in this case the outward look reveals a rather good taste.

On the other sides of the square there are other buildings, at times irregularly situated, with their colours faded by time, but warm in their tonality.

Church of St. Andrew

Just near the Herbs Square there is the small Mantegna Square, which is closely inserted into the historical centre of the town. The large and beautiful Church of St. Andrew faces this square.

This religious building is certainly one of the most important monuments representing the evolution of the artistic language of the 15th century and a very important stage of Renaissance art.

The Church was projected by Leon Battista Alberti (1404-1472), a renowned humanist and mainly a poet (if we may say so) of antiquity.

It is in the perspective of the recovery of the values of the classical world that one must interpret the architectonic solution which the artist carries out in his works, trying thus to renew the artistic canons. Notice how he repeats, thought not in a cold way, the schemes and motifs of classical antiquity (arches, pilaster strips, frontons, capitals, decorative elements, etc.) and mainly how he tries to recreate the sense of harmonious, perfect, balanced, solemn, measured space.

Perhaps this is the reason why he is a little abstract. But let us look at the structure of the church in detail.

Although the Basilica was projected by Alberti in 1470, it was

---

The monument to Virgil.

actually built by Luca Fancelli, who directed the works after the artist's death. The building was completed in the 16th century and partly in the 17th century. The dome was built by Filippo Juvara in the 18th century. The facade consists of three parts. In the centre there is a large arch including the entire height of the Church (the motif of this large arch recalls the triumphal arches of the Romans). On the outermost sections, the surface is underlined by windows and niches, while some half-pillars, crowned with capitals, separate it from the main body. A big gable rests on the facade, connecting all its various elements together. The same is true of the other large arch placed above the gable. Notice again that these are all motifs taken from the classical world. On the side of the Church is the powerful and elegant bell-tower in Gothic style.

Having passed through the entrance arch, we reach the vestibule with its elegant and beautiful lacunar ceiling. Then we come to the interior of the church. The interior consists of one large and imposing nave, on whose sides there are large chapels.

They are very deep and scanned: it was thus that Alberti solved, in a new and ingenious way, the traditional idea of the church with a nave and two aisles.

As a matter of fact, one gets the impression that the architecture is more articulated, and the whole is better structured, solemn and magnificent. And one gets such an impression not only from the size of the building, but also from the relations existing between the nave and the chapels, the balance among the various parts and some proportions (based on the geometrical figures of the sphere, circle and square), including, more than others, the concept of perfection and harmonious space, which can be measured by the humann eye.

The barrel-vault covering the nave and its chapels is also very beautiful. Less in harmony with the structure of the Church is the decoration carried out during the successive centuries. In fact, the architectonic elements of this building already include essential decorative elements, which do not need to be further embellished.

Let us look more in detail at the works which follow one another in the interior of the Church enriching it with various masterpieces.

We shall mention here only the most important ones.

1st chapel on the right: the Baptistery. In it we can also admire three beautiful works by Correggio: "The deposition of Jesus", "The Holy Family", "The Ascension of Christ" (the latter one was executed mainly by his assistants).

2nd chapel on the right: works by Andrea Pagni.

1st Chapel on the left: the beautiful tomb of Andrea Mantegna. Here the great artist was buried, who worked in Mantua for a long time, embellishing it with his masterpieces.

Notice, above the tomb, the bronze bust, perhaps made by Mantegna himself. The decoration of the chapel was also projected by the Master, but executed by him only in the part regarding the "Holy Family". His pupils and the sons themselves worked on other sections. Many other works are along the

The Rotunda of St. Laurence.

chapels of the nave and the transept.

Among the best ones we shall mention: the various 16th century mausoleums, among which of particular beauty are those by Strozzi and Andreasi; the fresco of the dome, made in the 18th century by Anselmi; some paintings by Lorenzo Costa the Younger (16th century); on the main altar is the relic of Christ's blood.

In 1572 it passed into the hands of Duke Guglielmo and at the beginning it was kept in the church of St. Barbara, till it was transferred to the present church, purposely built to honor it properly.

Then one can visit the **crypt** and get out from the back of the Church to enjoy an atmospheric view of the apse.

Having come back to the Herbs Square, going past the above mentioned Mayor's Palace, one reaches Broletto Square.

Here one can admire some interesting buildings, among which, beyond the facade itself of the Mayor's Palace, some 15th century palaces (notice that one whose facade still shows traces of frescoes), medieval houses, the "Arengario" and the very high **Tower of the Cage**, wich can be easily recognized by the cage above, where criminals were once kept.

The interior of the church of **St. Andrew**

The Church of St. Andrew.

Out of Broletto Square, through St. Peter's Arch, we reach the wonderful and atmospheric Sordello Square.

Thanks to the buildings facing it, this square has been the centre of the political, cultural and religious life of Mantua for a long time.

It is in this area that the first rulers of the town, the Bonacolsi, had their houses built, setting them into its medieval structure.

Later on, the Gonzaga, who ruled after the Bonacolsi, occupied their houses, enlarged them, building thus the Ducal Palace, which, for centuries, was the symbol of their political power and importance. And it was this noble and renowned family that projected Sordello Square, as it is today.

At the end of the 15th century the town-planning was renewed in order to have larger structures.

So various medieval houses and alleys were destroyed to create an area which corresponded better to the needs of the economic and social life of the town.

It is clear that such a great work of renewal and enlargement of the urban area was also meant to exalt the Gonzaga, who in this very square exercised their power, making it the real and ideal centre of their politics.

Now let us have a look at the buildings and monuments surrounding Sordello Square.

By the way, Sordello was a poet of Mantua, who is the author of a poem in Provençal, entitled "Tresor" (Treasure), and of a translation of the same poem into Italian, called "Tesoretto" (Little Treasure).

Sordello is mentioned also by Dante in his Divine Comedy.

On the left side of the square one can admire the ancient **medieval houses of the Acerbi and Bonacolsi**.

The latter's building dates back to the 13th century and has a beautiful battlement.

On the brick facade there is a simple but elegant series of windows.

At present the building is known as the Castiglioni Palace, because lived a noble family here, to which the famous Baldasar Castiglioni belonged.

He was of Mantuan origin, since he was born in Casatico, and belonged to the circle of those writers who worked in Mantua, as in other Italian courts, too. One of the fruits of his culture and long experience in such courts, was the "Courtier", a book where he outlines the ideal figure of the true courtier and courtesan, namely those who lived and worked at the courts of various noble families.

According to Castiglione, however, those figures represent the highest and noblest qualities of the ideal Renaissance man.

This is the reason for the enormous success of his book, which represents an era and its spiri-

Sordello Square

tuality.

The manuscript of Castiglione's book is kept in the archives of this Palace.

Immediately after the Bonacolsi House, there is the Baroque Bishop's House, not much in harmony with the architectonic taste of the other buildings of the square.

Between the two buildings one can see an atmospheric medieval alley.

The Cathedral faces the back of the square with its facade.

It was built at the beginning of the 12th century.

At the time it had a simple and linear Romanesque structure.

Of this remain, apart from the images handed down by an-cient prints, the bell tower and the right side.

The present building was constructed to a project by the architect Giulio Romano.

The facade was completed in the second half of the 18th century by Nicolò Baschiera and took the place of the old one in Gothic Style, badly damaged long since.

The unhappy result, however, is not in harmony with the medieval look, common to all the buildings of this square.

But let us consider the project by Giulio Romano more closely. It dates back to the middle of the 16th century, when the artistic tendencies and the architectonic solutions which were pre-

The Cathedral.

vailing during this period began to change.

The classical forms, which had permeated all of Renaissance art, were now animated by even stronger contrasts and deeper "chiaroscuros", pointing to a more complex spirituality, far from the serenity, harmony and perfection, which the man of the 15th-16th century thought he had found.

This subtle and new unrest, this spiritual crisis can also be seen in the architectonic lines, which many artists were experimenting with.

The interior of the Cathedral is a clear example of all this. In fact, with its classical lines and structure of the paleochristian basilicas, it still gives you a new sensation. It consists of five naves, but the side chapels almost form another two smaller naves. So the space tends to split up into various perspectives.

The sight of the whole is atmospheric indeed, and strikes the visitor with its solemnity and architectonic lines, with their lights and shades.

Observing more in detail the works of this wonderful interior, one can notice, first of all, the beautiful ceilings (lacunar and barrel ceilings) and the rich decoration of the walls. Beautiful paintings and sculptures embellish and make precious this church, which has become a true art gallery.

Among others we will mention here:

- The Chapel of Our Lady of the Coronation (15th century), a fine work by Luca Fancelli. Though various transformations have partly altered its structure, it still keeps an elegant and harmonious architectonic structure.
- Beautiful frescoes dating back to the 14th century (including a fine "*Crucifixion*") adorn the ceiling of the third chapel on the right.
- In the decoration of the other chapels and the transept, we recognize the hands of Bazzani, Brusasorci, Andreasino, Bedoli, Domenico Fetti, by whom a large fresco decorating the apse stands out.
- The *tapestries* of the Gonzaga family are beautiful as well.

On the right side of Sordello Square there is the facade of the magnificent Ducal Palace.

The interior of the Cathedral.

THE DUCAL PALACE

As a matter of fact, it is not only one palace, but consists of various buildings, which, erected and enlarged through the centuries, have formed a complex and regal structure.

It takes some hours to visit it properly, even limiting ourselves to the most important parts from the historical and artistic points of view. It is as if one were visiting a town enclosed in another town, so big is this palace, which is unique in Italy, at least from this point of view. The Ducal Palace gives the visitor an idea of the power reached by the Gonzaga family and how culture and art found in this court their natural cradle to express themselves as well as possible.

Those buildings, which now in Sordello Square are indicated as the Ducal Palace, were once the houses of the Bonacolsi, who, as we have already said, ruled the town of Mantua from 1273 to 1328. In fact, these palaces are very similar, as far as the outside structure is concerned, to those situated on the left side of the square. They are embattled buildings with porticoes. Elegant mullioned windows with two lights open on the facades. In the past they were known as the People's Captain's Palace and Domus Magna (Big House). When in 1328 the Gonzaga succeded the Bonacolsi in the government of the town, they also occupied their houses and lived in them for some time till they ordered some architects to transform and enlarge them.

The visitor has to go through various halls marked by Roman numbers. Each of them or a

group of them is indicated with a particular name generally referring to the decoration of the respective hall or to the name of the person who once occupied the apartment.

We do not want to make a long and perhaps boring list of names, but it is opportune to mention most of them for their architectonic and decorative value or for the events to which these halls are connected.

- The **Prince's Hall**: it is so called since various noblemen of the Gonzaga family are represented here. It is, however, better known as the **Pisanello Hall** because of the frescoes which were recently discovered here

The Ducal Palace.

(1969). These frescoes are worth considering in detail for their particular importance.

We can say here that it is a cycle of paintings dating back to the beginning of the 15th century and imitating sujects of the romances of chivalry and specially those of King Arthur's cycle. Knights, horses, ladies, arms, all find their place in a narrative structure recalling ancient fables.

One gets such an impression from those figures, which move and fight taking part in bloody duels and tournaments, but are as if immobilized in a world without atmosphere and history. As a matter of fact, that compact background behind the figures is neither air, nor sky, nor space: thus they emerge, beyond time and space, as if floating in an ageless world.

Pisanello was the poet of this fableland, of this courtly and chivalrous world, which could be narrated only by means of a fantastic transfiguration, full of nostalgia, or with the disenchantment suitable to all the beautiful

Pisanello Hall (a detail).

Pisanello Hall (a detail).

The Tapestries Apartment.

but unrepeatable things. This is the reason why Pisanello's painting became lyrical. It can be placed at the highest point of the late-Gothic experience, of which it reelaborates and interprets the main issues. Consequently, in most of the works by this artist, the main themes are dealt with in a very stylized and refined way. At the same time, but mainly during the last period of his activity, Pisanello showed humanistic tendencies, being more and more interested in things and men and using wider schemes for his designs and narrative structures. The frescoes of this hall which, as we have said, have been recently discovered, disappeared for a long time, damaged as they were by the collapse of the ceiling of this room.

A little after the Princes Hall we come to the - Apartments of Guastalla, which occupy six rooms of the old Captain's Palace, just behind the **Passerino Passage** (from the name of a member of the Bonacolsi Family). The above mentioned rooms, the residence of the Princess Isabella of Guastalla, were arranged between the end of the 16th century and the beginning of the 17th by the artist Viani. In all this section we often find traces of old frescoes dating back to the 14th century, once belonging to the decoration of the Bonacolsi palaces.

- The **New Gallery** was made by Viani. It contains many pictures once kept in various halls of the palace.

After some rooms one reaches the **Apartment of the Tapestries**, so called for the tapestries kept here, representing a precious artistic patrimony. They (nine in all) were executed to

The Rivers Hall.
Pensile Garden.

designs by Raphael Sanzio and constitute one of the first copies of them. They represent important episodes in the life of saints Peter and Paul. The Apartment of Tapestries (once known as the Green Apartment and re-structured by the architect Antonio Maria Viani) was realized as it is now in the second half of the 18th century by the artist Paolo Pozzo by order of the Austrian Empire, which ruled the town since the beginning of that century.

Then come other halls which take their name from the subjects of the frescoes kept in them. Among them: - **The hall of the Rivers**, with a beautiful decoration by Anselmi; - **the Pensile Garden**, an elegant work dating back to the 16th century. It is an open and quiet place, with a light portico resting on double columns. The lawn and hedges create fine and complex geometrical designs.

In the following halls one can admire rich and precious tapestries and elegant furniture.

After the **Passage of the Months** (with its typical 17th century decoration) one reaches the long **Hall of Mirrors**, luxurious and striking, thanks to its rich decorations dating back to the 17th and 18th centuries, part of which are taken from designs by A. M. Viani.

- **The Archers' Hall**, so called because in this room the archers mounting guard at the ducal apartment, of which this hall was the antechamber were stationed. The **Ducal Apartment**: it includes an interesting series of halls realized by order of Duke Guglielmo Gonzaga in the 16th century and completed during the following centuries mainly by Viani himself. Among them

The Mirrors Hall.
The Archers Hall.

33

we shall mention here the **Labyrinth Hall**, recognizable for the original decoration of its ceiling, representing a labyrinth on which a sentence pronounced by Duke Vincenzo I during the siege of Canissa, is inscribed ("forse che si, forse che no", that is "maybe yes, maybe no"). Notice a little further on after the **Ladder of Paradise**, the fine and ingenious small **Apartment of the Dwarfs**, easily recognizable since all its rooms have been built in proportion to the height of the dwarfs.

Then one goes through the **Bertani Passage** and the **Apartment of Metamorphoses** (by the architect A. M. Viani), the old seat of the Gonzaga Library. Then one reaches the **Rustica** (or Summer Apartment): the building shows, in its interior, interesting architecture with quite original and new features. It was projected by Giulio Romano, who worked in Mantua in the first half of the 16th century. For this building he wanted to try rustic ashlar-work, with rough squared stones, which gave a rustic look to it, hence its name. The summer apartment (this is the name of the series of rooms we are visiting now) was probably the summer residence of the Gonzaga family themselves. It includes six rooms, which open partly onto the Exhibition Courtyard (or Horsewoman's Courtyard), and partly face the Lower Lake.

Onto the same **Exhibition Courtyard** (an original work by Bertani who, imitating the syle of the Rustica, re-elaborated it in a very personal way), opens the wonderful **Exhibition Gallery**. It was built by order of duke Vincenzo Gonzaga, taking

The Labyrinth Hall.

the place of various rooms, which once were along the long side of the building. Here the duke exhibited his wonderful collections of precious objects. The ceiling is very beautiful and also quite interesting are the sculptures placed in the niches along the walls. The shorter side of the same building (facing the Exhibition Courtyard) is occupied by the **Gallery of the Months**. Before it one sees the Summer Apartment. From one

Rubens - The Trinity in Glory.

34

side there is a sweeping view across the lake.

Other rooms are situated at the back of the Church of St. Barbara (of which we shall speak later). These, too, are particularly beautiful thanks to their decorations and interesting thanks to historical and cultural testimonies kept in them.

These rooms include the properly called Ducal Palace, and at the same time connect it to St. George's Castle, of which it is an inseparable complement.

Among the various rooms of this section we mention here the **Hall of Troy** with decorations dating back to the 16th century and representing some episodes of the Trojan war; the **Caesars' Hall**, with copies of the portraits of the Caesars executed by Titian; some rooms built by Giulio Romano and Bertani; the **Loggia of Tasso**, so called because it seems that the poet Torquato Tasso stayed here when he was freed from the prison where he had been put after he had been seized by a fit of anger; The **Hall of Apollo**, with a beautiful stucco frieze by Primaticcio (16th century); the **Captain's Hall**, where the busts of the dukes of the Gonzaga family are kept (the decoration of the room, too, is very beautiful); **Manto's Hall**: here the frescoes narrate the legend of the foundation of Mantua by Manto. This hall is particularly atmospheric for its magnificent decoration, perhaps executed by Primaticcio and the magnificence of the room itself.

From this hall ascends a great staircase, known as **Aeneas's Staircase**, executed in the 16th century by the architect Bertani, which connects the Ducal Palace to St. George's Castle.

The Exhibition Courtyard.
The Exhibition Gallery.

Manto's Hall.

ST. GEORGE'S CASTLE

This magnificent fortification work was done by Bartolino of Novara at the end of the 14th century.

As the walls of Mantua, it met the need of the Gonzaga family to defend the town and their domination, thus strengthening their power.

At that time defensive works were particularly important and efficacious: the town was all closed by fortifications, which were added to the natural ones constituted by the lakes surrounding it. The structure of the Castle is massive and imposing: it is quadrangular and animated by four powerful towers. In the past it was surrounded by a moat.

Through the centuries it has been often restructured and transformed, but substantially it

has kept the shape and look of a powerful stronghold.

St. George's Bridge, starting from the Castle, crosses the Middle and Lower Lakes, indicating ideally their limits.

The outward look of the Castle can be observed in detail once one gets out of it.

But having interrupted our itinerary in its interior, we shall go on describing the various rooms from where we interrupted it, namely from Aeneas' Hall.

Notice, first of all, the beautiful **Courtyard**, an example of elegant and simple Renaissance architecture, attributed to Mantegna or to Fancelli, and by others to Laurana himself.

In the interior of the Castle we shall have the opportunity of admiring one of the greatest examples of the Italian art of the 15th century, namely Mantegna's paintings.

We come to, first of all, the **Entrance Hall**. It is a large room frescoed with subjects taken from paintings by Mantegna himself, but executed by other artists. Further on, after some

St. George's Castle.

The Room of the Married Couple.

The Room of the Married Couple.

The Room of the Married Couple - Oeil-de-boeuf.   The Meeting. ➤

less important rooms, one reaches the renowned **Room of the Married Couple**.

Known in the past mainly as the "Camera picta", this hall, completely painted by Andrea Mantegna, represents one of the most significant masterpieces of Italian art and also the moment of the highest creativity and maturity of the artist.

In order to understand better his way of expressing himself and appreciate all the beauty of this room, it is better to examine it in detail and to give some information about the life and the cultural formation of the artist who executed it.

Andrea Mantegna, born around 1430/1421 in Padua, in a poor family, was entrusted while still very young to the painter Francesco Squarcione so that he might work with him.

It was there that the boy learned to paint and love art.

Very soon he revealed exceptional qualities and his creative sensibility. Imagine that he was

only 17 when he was ordered to paint, in Padua, the Ovetari Chapel.

So he very soon became a famous and requested artist. He worked in Ferrara and Verona.

In 1459 he was called to Mantua by duke Lodovico in order to paint the Gonzaga Chapel.

He came back there after some time to paint the above mentioned Room of the Married Couple. Those were the years from 1471 to 1474, when he reached his highest point of maturity.

He worked again in Mantua under duke Francesco II, for whom he painted "Caesar's Triumph". (Nothing now remains in Mantua of this cycle of paintings.

The Triumphs, together with other masterpieces which embellished the Ducal Palace, were sold by duke Vincenzo II Gonzaga at the beginning of the 17th century, and ever since they have embellished the museums of London and Paris.

This cycle of paintings is now in London and its state of conservation is not at all good.

The magnificient painting clled "Caesar's Triumph" had a great success and favourably impressed many artists of the time, so much so that many of them were inspired by it and even imitated it).

Then he went to Rome where he painted the Chapel of Pope Innocent VIII.

The activity of this great artist went on continually till his death in 1506.

His painting represented a very important stage in Renaissance culture.

Mantegna was educated at Squarcione's school, but he was also influenced by many other schools and artistic currents.

But he received his most important lessons from the classical world.

This world was for him particularly valuable, full as it was of harmony and beauty.

This is the reason why he exalted it, but in a nostalgic way, because he perceived that nothing could relive completely.

He was also influenced by many artists working in Padua, and most of all, by Donatello, who was also an admirer of the classical world and of that humanity which looked so heroic and dignified.

Mantegna was also influenced by Bellini and all the other artists he knew and admired during his many travels.

Mantegna's painting shows elements which can be easily identified: the figures, though quite realistic, reveal a certain monumentality, by which the strength and dignity of the Renaissance man are affirmed, and particular techniques, such as the use of a lower point of view, whereby the figures themselves are seen in perspective from the bottom upwards.

In the narrative structure, as in the other important elements of his painting, the classical world emerges very clearly; but not so much in the representation found quite frequently in Mantegna, made of pieces of columns or arches set into the scenes as if they were archaeological finds, but rather in the plasticity and the ample, solemn vision of the scenes themselves.

We must admit, however, that Mantegna never follows the classical models slavishly.

His was rather an anguished and nostalgic adhesion, because it was impossible to recreate it.

Mantegna's portrait.

Therefore his representations are permeated by melancholy and poetic accents.

He was also the poet of present time, of reality: courts and courtiers have, thanks to him, a completely earthly character, which the refinement and splendour of their life and condition never altered.

Mantegna is also the creator of new and daring insights (an example is the ceiling of the Room of the Married Couple, and the first one of its kind), which open onto aerial and atmospheric perspectives.

This was an element which noticeably influenced Italian painting during the successive centuries.

But it is time to examine in detail the Room of the Married Couple, now that we have a key to understanding it better.

Its decoration was completed between 1471 and 1474, but we do not know whether he went on working at these paintings continually.

There is also a great deal of discussion as regards the unity of his period of inspiration. As a matter of fact, an accurate examination reveals some inconsistencies and at times small contradictions, which should be examined in more detail. However, this is not the place to do so. It is enough for now to bear in mind his work as a whole and all its characteristics. The room is not very large and probably was used as a delegation hall.

The **ceiling** of the room is decorated with stuccoes and shows eight medallions. In the middle, with a rich floral ornament, opens the "**oeil-de-boeuf**".

It is an ingenious solution created by Mantegna, quite new for those times. The artist paints this part of the ceiling imagining the observer who, situated in the centre of the room, looks above.

Thus he provides a sort of aerial vision in which everything - the fake banister, the objects, the people - is put into perspective.

Certainly it represents a masterpiece of ability and shows a clear determination to draw the attention, but we are still far from the refinements and hyperbole characterizing the aerial perspectives in the 17th and 18th centuries.

Notice also that on the ceiling, as on the other walls, Mantegna wanted to create fake architecture, which creates particular optical effects.

For instance, see how the ceiling, thanks to fake architectonic elements, looks more convex than it is in reality, while the columns and pillars painted along the walls create deeper perspectives and, at the same time, set the scenes in a more real and tangible environment.

Other paintings are in the **lunettes**.

There are 12 altogether, and many of them have been damaged. The subjects are various: animals, plants and emblems.

Let us examine now the **walls** along which Mantegna wanted to glorify the Gonzaga family. **North wall**: it is the main one, where the fire-place is.

It represents the Gonzaga court: Ludovico Gonzaga is sitting (he is the one who ordered the work) turned towards his secretary Andreasi. Barbara of Bandeburg, his wife, sits in a frontal position, and, between them, their children Federico, Ludovico and Paola.

On the right side, just as if he is coming out of the drape of Bar-

The Meeting - detail of the landscape.

bara's dress, is the very realistic portrait of the court dwarf.

Other figures are represented along the wall, forming thus a harmonious, plastic representation.

Not all the personages have been identified and so only conjectures can be put forward.

The **east wall** and the **south wall** are painted with fake curtains, which Mantegna imagines as if gathered and supported by a wall, so as to create the illusion that one uncovers the stories of the other walls by lifting them up. Notice also the precious and refined ornaments characterizing these draperies.

As a matter of fact, it seems that these walls were once really covered with leather curtains, probably very similar to those represented by Mantegna.

The **west wall**: it is divided into three sections, but there is only one scene.

It represents the meeting between Ludovico Gonzaga and his son Francesco, the cardinal. The main scene of the meeting is represented on the right side of the wall, and here, too, various personages of the court and retinue can be recognized.

Ludovico is represented in profile, advancing respectfully towards his son, who, in this case, represents the ecclesiastical authority. The latter, wearing his cardinal's dress, is placed in the foreground so as to stress the importance of his office.

Other personages of the Gonzaga family are quite recognizable, but not always.

Moreover, Mantegna has represented himself on the right side: he is the violet dressed figure, in an almost frontal position, in the group immediately behind the cardinal.

In the background a town is represented, probably Rome, rich in wonderful monuments and full of life.

The central part of this wall shows paintings of dogs and putti supporting an inscription with the dedication of this painting to Ludovico Gonzaga and his wife by Mantegna. The year (1474) is indicated, in which the artist completed his work.

In the left section a horse, some dogs and waiting servants are represented. Some critics have thought this to be a distinct scene, a sort of "Return from hunting". As a matter of fact, the whole scene on this wall is so closely connected in its various parts and so logical in its narration, that it does not need to be considered separate from the rest.

Notice, in the background, the beautiful landscape rich in vegetation in the foreground, but bare and rocky in the background. Fortified towns rise on the rocky peaks.

The detailed description of this room and the subjects here painted, should not make us forget the importance of the decoration as a whole, nor, above all, the complex and solemn structure of its various parts, the plasticity and harmony of the whole.

The court and its characters are painted by Mantegna as if set into their aulic and splendid world, seen as they are as important people, but also as real people, living on this earth.

The artist represents their faces with realism, without idealizing them, but, with a sharp spirit of observation, reveals the tendencies of their character and their defects. And though at times he idealizes his landscape, real life returns in the architectonic structure of the scenes.

All this creates a solemn and, at the same time, harmonious effect, which is the measure itself of Mantegna's art.

Let us come back now to the other rooms of St. George's Castle:The **Hall of the Grotto**, where Isabella of Este lived. Particularly beautiful is the ceiling in carved wood.

The **Arms Hall** and the **Palaelogue's Room** (almost completely re-built): in these rooms there are frescoes by Giulio Romano, which were later touched up and repaired.

On the second floor of the Castle are the political prisons, recalling the names of many men of the Italian Risorgimento, who fought for the unity and independence of Italy.

In the Castle one can still visit **Isabella's Apartment**.

She is Isabelle of Este who, while still very young, married Francesco Gonzaga. She had come from the court of Ferrara, splendid for its Maecenatism and cultural interests.

In Mantua, too, she tried to encourage and foster, in any way possible, the formation of a cultural and artistic area, which would make the town important

The Basilica of St. Barbara.

and reach the cultural level of other courts.

Isabella gathered rich collections of pictures and ceramics. Among the works patronized by her, there is the **Little Study**, which has a very beautiful wooden ceiling (we have seen a similar one in the Hall of the Grotto).

The Little Study, transferred many times, was the place where Isabella used to with-draw. For this room fine pictorial works were executed by Man-tegna, Lorenzo Costa, Perugino, while many other artists were consulted for its decoration.

Unfortunately, the works which embellished it are now kept in various museums all over the world, and so it is impossible to appreciate the beauty and ele-gance of this room as a whole.

Isabella's Rooms, which till the beginning of the 16th century occupied this area of the Castle, were dismantled and rebuilt where we now find them. Here, however, we can still see the fine **garden** built at the beginning of the 16th century by order of Isabella herself.

From Isabella's Apartment one can get out to Sordello Square. The **Basilica of St. Barbara**, too, is a part of the palace. It was built by order of the Gonzaga family as their personal church.

The author of the projects was Bertani, who began to built it around 1562.

The facade has three high arches leading into a presbytery.

On the right side there is a beautiful bell-tower, which is quite original in terms of its architectonic structure, animated as it is by lines culminating on high in an ingenious cylindrical solution, made lighter by airy arches resting on double columns.

The interior seems to have been influenced by the pursuit of new and striking effects.

What strikes you is mainly that play of light which, coming down from the large windows of the dome, flows on the walls creating effects of sharp luminous contrasts and developing a dialogue which goes beyond a simple architectonic quest.

In the interior we can admire some works by Lorenzo Costa, Brusasorci, and a *"Crucifix"* by Gianbologna (kept in the Sacristy).

Once out of the Church, one can visit the **Square of Paradise**, the Square of the Lombard League and the **Pavilion Gardens**, all belonging to the Ducal Palace.

Courtyard of Honour.
Pavilion Garden.

3rd Route:

North-West Section: From St. George's Bridge to the Mills Bridge, to Pradella Gate Square.

This short route includes that part of the town which extends to the west of the Herbs Square and Sordello Square, towards the Middle and Upper Lakes.

One can come from Mantegna Square or Broletto Square or sordello Square or St. George's Castle. We indicate the latter one as the beginning of the present route in order to connect us to our previous route and then follow it in a more harmonious and rational way.

From St. George's Bridge overlooking the Tower and Middle Lakes, we can go along a long stretch of Mincio Avenue, which runs straight along the Middle Lake.

We reach thus the magnificient **Virgilian Square**.

It was structured by the architect Paolo Pozzo and completed towards the end of the 18th century under the patronage of the Frenchmen, who ruled Mantua at that time, during a brief break in the Austrian domination.

This square was structured a little after the reclamation of a marshy area occupying this large area and its environs.

In its background there is the **Monument to Virgil**, by the sculptor Luca Beltrami. (We recall here that Virgil was a Latin poet of Mantuan origin, since he was born in ancient Andes). On the right side of the same square (with your back to Viale Mincio) are the barracks of the "Carabinieri", in whose interior one can admire some beautiful Renaissance cloisters, remains of an ancient 15th century building.

A little after, along Zambelli Street, we find the **Church of St.. Leonard**.

It is a very old building, since it dates back to the 12th century. Of this period only the beautiful belfry remains, with its simple and linear shape.

This religious building is contemporary with the Cathedral of Mantua and it has been almost completely destroyed.

In its interior we can still admire some fine paintings, including one of particular interest by

Lorenzo Costa and one by Francia.

Turning a little further and taking Cavriari Street, we find the **Cavriari Palace** (18th century). Then we walk towards the **Mills Bridge** (built around 1990), separating the Middle Lake from the Upper Lake.

It was built when the Mincio was reclaimed and its waters regulated by order of Alberto Pitentino. It is preceded by the **Molina Gate**, one of the five gates along the walls which closed the town (the others are St. George's, Pradell, Pusterla and Cerese gates).

Then one can follow Pitentino Street, along which the railway runs, crossing the Mills Bridge itself after a while.

One can also take Portazzolo Street leading directly to C. d'Arco Square, where the d'**Arco Palace** rises. It is a building in neo-classical style.

The front body, as far as the exedra, was built in 1784 and during the following years by the architect Antonio Colonna who, especially in the lines of the facade, was inspired by Palladio's art.

The building was owned by the Counts of D'Arco of Trent, who since 1740 had partly settled in

The Virgilian Square - the monument to Virgil.

D'Arco palace.

Mantua, where they had inherited the Counts Chieppo's house. In 1780 Giovan Battista Gherardo D'Arco charged Antonio Colonna with the complete rebuilding of the preexisting palace.

One century later, another member of that family, Count Francesco Antonio D'Arco, bought, from the Marquises Della Valle, the area situated beyond the exedra and including some Renaissance buildings, and the garden, thus enlarging the old residence of the Chieppo family.

More recently the Palace, which houses furniture, pantings and other objects of great artistic value, has been transformed into a public museum at the request of Giovanna of the Counts D'Arco.

The first hall we come to, in the interior of the building, is that of the Ancestors, so called because in it are kept 60 portraits of various members of the D'Arco family. The portraits, all executed between the 16th and the 18th century, were once in Trent and later were transferred to Mantua.

From the Ancestors Hall one has access to the other halls.

On the left side there are the rooms that in the last century formed the private quarters of the owners of the palace; on the left side there are the Halls of the picture-gallery.

On the right side we find the Hall of the architectonic perspectives, adorned with elegant neo-classical decorations and furniture dating back partly to the 18th century and partly to the first half of the 19th century; the Portraits Hall, with 18th century to the first half of the 19th century; the Still

Life Hall, that was once the dining-room and contains a table laid with 18th century crockery; the little Loggia, a very beautiful room adorned with fine decorations and various sculptures; the Music Hall, where a collection of musical instruments is kept.

From the Ancestors Hall, turning to the left, we get into the Picture-Gallery which includes seven halls.

The first hall is Diana's Room, so named after the representations on the vault.

Of great interest is a painting of Caravaggio's school representing *Joseph and Potiphar's wife*, the figure of a satyr, attributed to Bartolomeo Manfredi of Cremona, a painting representing "*Juno, Ceres and Psyche*", by Sante Peranda of Venice. "*The rich man's supper*", executed in the 16th century, and a painting of Carracci's school of Bologna, representing "*Jupiter and Antiope*".

Then comes the Red Hall, a typical example of an aristocratic room in the second half of the 19th century.

It contains furniture, paintings and wonderful objects of porcelain and silver. In the middle of the hall is the portrait of Count Francesco Antonio D'Arco, by whose order all the furniture in this room was made.

Then we enter Pallas Hall. Its lacunar ceiling is very beautiful; in the middle there is the image of wisdom, after which the hall is named. On the walls there are some 16th-17th century paintings, mostly portraits.

Noteworthy are the portrait of a lady dressed in black, atributed to Girolamo Forabosco, the image of a friar, by Jacob Denys, a Fleming; the portrait of Vincent I Gonzaga, the duke of Mantua, and on old copy of the portrait of Baldassar Castiglione executed by Raphael and today kept in the Louvre Museum.

There are some extremely beautiful portraits of ladies. 18th century furniture and 16th-17th century Flemish paintings adorn the Green Hall or Hall of Justice, where there is also a fine work dating back to the second half of the 15th century and representing the "*Madonna with the Child and Angels*".

Near it is the Neo-classical Hall, adorned with stuccoes and neoclassical ornaments.

From the Green Hall one reaches the Hall of the Sacred Representations, where mostly religious paintings are kept.

The furniture dates back to the 17th and 18th centuries. Among the many works kept here, worthy of note are: "*Christ bearing the cross*", executed in the 16th century, attributed to Maineri, "*St. Jerome*" by Bartolomeo Montagna; a "*Deposition*" by Rubens' school; "*Christ's Flagellation*" by Lorenzo Costa the Younger; "*Christ ascending to Heaven*"; atributed to Lorenzo Lotto; a fine "*Crucifix*" by Van Dyck's school; a "*Madonna*" by the 16th century Umbrian school; "*Christ bearing the cross*", attributed to Sodoma (16th century).

Then we reach the Passage of the Reliquaries, where each case contains a fine collection of reliquaries, and the Hall of Alexander the Great or Bassani Hall. This hall is named after the seven large paintings representing episodes in the life of Alexander the Great.

These paintings, by Giuseppe Bazzani of Mantua (18th century), represent from right to left: Alexander while receiving the mother of Darius, the king of Persia; Alexander with his horse Bucephalus; Alexander with soothsayers; Alexander with Darius' family; Alexander at the deathbed of Darius' wife; Alexander the Great meets his future wife, Roxana; Alexander's and Roxana's wedding.

In the same hall there are some Renaissance and 18th century works.

As we have already said, behind the main buildings of the palace, beyond the garden, there are other architectonic buildings, among which the most interesting one is what remains of a construction dating back to the end of the 15th century.

There are some rooms of the original construction, namely three rooms on the ground floor and a very large one on the upper floor.

Now we come to the ground floor, where there are two halls and a chapel. The first hall has pensile capitals and amphorae of the Roman period; it also contains religious paintings and the paintings and the genealogical tree of the Agnelli family of Mantua.

In the second hall there are some paintings, among which one by Giovan Battista Venanti (16th century), representing the Magi visiting the Child Jesus. Two small tables support some 17th century niches.

A door, surmounted by a painting by Cignaroli, with the Madonna, the Child and Saints, leads into the chapel containing a 17th century marble altar, a beautiful altar frontal of Morocco leather, and ancient vestments. On the upper floor of the building there is the large Hall of the Zodiac.

The Hall of the Zodiac, entirely adorned with frescoes, is a wonderful example of humanistic culture. The pictorial work, executed around the year 1520 by Giovan Battista Falconetto of Verona, is inspired by the theme of the Zodiac, hence the name of the hall.

It illustrates myths and legends concerning the constellations. The walls are divided into twelve panels separated by pil-

lars and surmounted by friezes. Each panel represents a sign of the Zodiac.

The paintings also represent ancient buildings of various Italian towns, such as the Coliseum in Rome, Theodoric's Mausoleum and the church of St. Vita in Ravenna. A panel, the one showing Libra to be precise, was destroyed in the 17th century, when the large fire-place, situated at the end of the hall, was

Hall of the Zodiac.

built. Near it there is an iron case with its lid lifted to allow visitors to see its lock, which is truly extraordinary in its ingenuity.

From the Hall of the Zodiac we proceed into the garden, and from here into the kitchen built in the 19th century.

Copper, brass and pewter cooking vessels, all in good order, are kept in this kitchen. Indeed, throughout the museum, the furniture, paintings and other objects are situated in the same rooms and in the same places as before the death of Giovanna d'Arco. Near this palace we can see the remains of the Renaissance **Della Valle Palace**. In one of its halls there are some beautiful wall paintings executed by G. M. Falconetto, representing allegories of the signs of the Zodiac.

From D'Arco Square, through Fernelli Strett, one reaches the 17th century **Canossa Palace**. From the same square, but taking Scarsellini Street, we can reach the interesting **Church of St. Francis** situated in the homonymous square.

It is a beautiful building, probably dating back to the beginning of the 14th century.

Though it was almost completely destroyed by a bombardment during the last war, it has recently been restored to its original shape. The church faces the square with its monumental Gothic facade.

Its brick structure gives this building an austere and solemn look, harmoniously combined with the simplicity of the Franciscan architecture.

The two pilaster strips vertically dividing the facade indicate the division, into a nave and two aisles, of the interior. A beautiful rose window and a portal adorn it in a simple and sober way.

Three smalls spires, in the form of belfries, are situated on high, in the triangulation formed by the roof. Delicate crowning, with small pensile arches, completes the simple decoration.

The interior, too, is simple and austere, thanks also to its brickwork. In the nave and the two aisles, which are quite ample and harmonious, there are some interesting paintings and sculpture, dating back mostly to the 14th century.

But its finest part is certainly the **Gonzaga Chapel**, built under the patronage of the rulers of Mantua in the second half of the 14th century. The architecture is balanced, harmonious and very simple.

Of great interest are its frescoes representing *scenes in the life of Christ*, *St. Francis* and other saints. Its author was Tommaso of Modena, but other artists worked on it, though their identity is not certain.

Stefano da Verona, too, worked in this church, and painted "*St. Francis receiving the stigmata*".

We should remember, however, that this, along with other works, is now kept in the Ducal Palace,

to prevent them from being further damaged, since the church was seriously damaged by various bombardments.

Moreover, the paintings in this church represent the few medieval paintings still present in Mantua. A little after the church, there is **St. Francis' Bridge**, which crosses the Rio (an internal canal crossing Mantua transversally), where it meets the Upper Lake.

Pitentino Street, running beyond Don Leoni Square, where the railway station is, reaches Pradella Gate Square, where one of the most ancient gates of the town once stood.

Hall of the Zodiac.

4th Route:

North-East Section : From Sordello Square to the Virgilian Academy, Porto Catena, Belfiore Martyrs Square.

Taking the Herbs Square and Sordello Square as reference points and going towards the Lower Lake, one reaches first Dante Square and then the **Virgilian Academy** and the **Theatre of The Academy**. These buildings date back to the 18th century.

It was the period in which the town of Mantua, after the decline of the Gonzaga family, was involved in a new political situation.

Mantua, like most of Italy, lost its independence and passed under the direct rule of the Austrian Empire.

But, though it lost its autonomy and freedom, its cultural and artistic life did not decline, thanks also to the empress Maria Teresa.

It was in this historical period and under such a patronage that, in the second half of the 18th century, the Theatre of the Academy and then the Academy itself were built.

The Theatre (situated on the first floor of the Virgilian Academy) was projected by the architect Antonio Bibbiena. It is a small but fine and harmonious masterpiece.

Its architecture still shows Baroque influences, but the whole is quite balanced and sober, without any striking effect. The Virgilian Academy was the seat of the Royal Academy of Sciences and Art.

The building which, as we have already said, includes the Theatre itself, was transformed in the second half of the 18th century by the architect Giuseppe Piermarini, who created a balanced and harmonious structure.

Near it, but a little further south, we find other important buildings, such as the **State Archives**, rich in important records, including those belonging to the Gonzaga family, the **Library**, built under the patronage of the Austrian empress, and some medieval houses and towers.

A little further on there is the **Finance Palace**, on whose 18th

Sordi Palace.
The Scientific Theatre.

century facade Paolo Pozzo worked, an architect who worked in Mantua for a long time and re-arranged the Virgilian Square.

Near it, along Pompanazzo Street, there is **Sordi Palace**. It is a typical example of Baroque architecture.

It was built in the second half of the 17th century by the Flemish architect Geffels, according to artistic tendencies quite widespread at that time.

Though the outside structure of the palace shows clear Baroque lines, the whole is quite simple, without any striking effect.

In the interior, however, there are many pictorial and stucco decorations, which spoil its various rooms (built by Gian Battista Berberini). Notice also the Courtyard and the Staircase, quite sumptuous thanks to many sculptural groups.

Going along the same Pompanazzo Street southward, one finds the **Church of St. Martin** and then **Catena Harbour**. This harbour was made when the Gonzaga built St. George's fortress, creating thus a safe shelter for boats and, at the same time, completing the arrangement of the town.

The **Rio** begins at Catena Harbour and is a small canal which crosses the town transversely before flowing into the Upper Lake. This small canal, which was probably built towards the 12th century, crosses most of the oldest area of Mantua, running among the houses and passing under small bridges.

In this way it creates an atmospheric and picturesque landscape, quite similar to some corners of Venice.

From Catena Harbour, crossing Fondamenta Street and then Corridoni Street, one reaches the Belfiore Martyrs Square. During this walk it is possible to admire the town and above all the many buildings along these streets.

In this way one can acquire a better knowledge of Mantua's town-planning, which was always characterized by good taste and nobility.

The **Belfiore Martyrs Square** is dedicated to those men who, with their patriotic zeal and the sacrifice of their lives, honoured the town during the fights for the independence of Mantua and Lombardy from Austrian domination.

It is a central area of the town and the meeting point of many roads. Froma one side one can see the Rio, in which a fine portico is reflected.

A high **bell-tower** dominates the square: it is that of the **Church of St. Dominic**, which, built towards the middle of the 14th century for the Dominican Order, was completely lost.

At the foot of the bell-tower one can admire the so called **Pescherie**, built by the architect Giulio Romano.

As for other buildings of the town, this artist used rustic ashlar-work, which in this work of his can be seen only partially, since only the portices are still standing.

On another side of the square there is the main Post Office.

From this square, taking Roma Street, one passes near the Town Hall (19th century) and reaches Mantegna Square. Along these streets one can admire some houses dating back to the 14th and 15th centuries.

Through Grazioli Street, which leaves the square at the level of the Post Office, one reaches the

nearby Cavallotti Square, where the **Social Theatre** is.
It was built by Luigi Canonica in the first half of the 19th century.

Its architectonic structure is quite similar to that of the best known theatres of that time. Its style is clearly neo-classical. In

The Rio.

its interior there is a long row of boxes.

Even today many performances and concerts take place here, bearing witness to a long and appreciated cultural tradition.

Umberto Avenue leads off Cavallotti Square and runs as far as Marconi Square.

Notice the classical porticoes, under which there are many shops and where people promenade. G. Arrivabene Street and Ippolito Nievo Street run northward till they meet the Virgilian Square.

Lastly G. Marangari Street leads towards the Church of St. Francis, while Vittorio Emanuele Avenue, passing near the 17th century **Church of St. Ursula**, the **Andreasi Theatre** and the **Church of All Saints** (18th century), reaches Pradella Gate Square.

Belfiore Martyrs Square.
The Social Theatre.

5th Route:

The Southern Quarters - From the Belfiore Martyrs Square to the Tea Palace.

Taking as reference point the central Belfiore Martyrs Square, we go now towards the southern area of the town. The Ciassi Street which starts from here, having run along the 16th century **Aldegatti Palace**, which has an elegant portal, reaches the **Church of St. Mauritius** built in the 17th century by the architect Antonio Maria Viani, who also built other houses, including the famous Palace of the Gonzaga of Vescovato, of which we shall speak later. In the interior of the Church we can admire some paintings by Ludovico Carracci, Bazzani and Denys.

Going along the same Chiassi Street, one turns to the left, at the level of Carlo Poma Street. Then we come to two interesting buildings: the houses of Giulio Romano and the **Church of St. Barnabas**.

The Church of St. Barnabas: it was built by the architect Moscatelli, who projected it at the beginning of the 18th century shaping it in quite an original way, as we can see in the interior with a single nave.

The facade was built by Antonio Bibiena.

As we have said, the interior has only one nave and some interesting works by Lorenzo Costa and Giuseppe Bazzani.

Of the latter we shall mention mainly the beautiful painting representing "St. Romuald" (now situated in the Sacristy), one of the best works of this artist. In it the use of the light-effect tends to create an evocative atmosphere, suitable for the theme of the painting, which is that of the "vision", the "dream".

You should also have a look at what remains of the **Cloister**, built in the simple and harmonious style of the Renaissance.

A little further on we come to the **House of Giulio Romano**. It was the artist's house for the whole period he stayed in Mantua.

The building, already existing, was re-structured and decorated by him, according to his taste and architectonic and pictorial canons.

Giulio Romano (that is Giulio Pippi, born in Roma in 1492) had arrived at this town around 1524, brought here by Baldassarre Castiglione himself.

He remained in Mantua for the rest of his life working continually and leaving here many works, among which the Rustica, the Tea Palace, the Pescherie, the Cathedral, the Church of St. Dominic, apart from various paintings adorning the buildings themselves.

Considering the number of his works and the elements characterizing them, he has left in this town the mark of a taste and a style, which could easily be followed by other artists.

The house of Giulio Romano is characterized, as are his other works, by the use of rustication.

In its architecture, as well as in the decoration of the interior, we perceive the preferences of the artist, who uses exuberant ornamental motifs and solutions to great effect. Since he was educated at Raphael's school, he likes to repeat classical motifs,

Mantegna's House.

at times full of a certain academism or monumentality, at times more balanced and harmonious.

Then we walk along Carlo Poma Street, go beyond a 16th century building, perhaps projected by Giulio Romano (a beautiful *"Madonna with Child"* in terracotta adorns its facade) and reach the **Palace of Justice** or **Palace of the Gonzaga of Vescovato** (from the name of a side branch of the Gonzaga family). It was built by Antonio Maria Viani at the beginning of the 17th century; it is imposing and scenographic. The long front of the palace rests on a powerful rusticated base.

The upper part, where the rustication is less protruding, is marked by big semi-pillars, on which the caryatids rest.

The play of the architectonic masses is of great effect, mainly thanks to the plastic movement of the supporting stuctures. The interior is rich and sumptuous.

The decoration (notice particularly the frescoes representing "Boar Hunting") can be attributed to Viani himself.

Then we proceed to where Poma Street, Prince Amedeo Street (connected to the Belfiore Martyrs Square), Giulio Romano Avenue (leading to the eastern quarters of the town) and Giovanni Acerbi Street meet.

The latter leads to **Mantegna's House**.

It dates back to the second half of the 15th century. It was Ludovico Gonzaga himself, for whom Mantegna painted the room of the Married Couple, that donated the land to the artist.

Perhaps the painter himself projected this house, but it cannot be proved.

We notice, however, a certain resemblance between this building and the above mentioned Room, as far as some architectonic solutions and their plastic configuration are concerned. From this point of view, we can consider the original inside **courtyard**, cylindrical, atmospheric and harmonious, and compare it with the "eye" painted on the ceiling of the Room of the Married Couple.

It has a circular form, which, in both cases, is set into a cubic form (that of the house and the room). If all this is not enough to attribute also to Mantegna the project of his house, it is the ingeniousness and the peculiarity of the solution adopted which lead us to think of a single creative mind.

Not far from Mantegna's House is the beautiful **Church of St. Sebastian**.

The author of this interesting and fine project was Leon Battista Alberti, the same artist who projected the church of St. Andrew.

The works began in the latter half of the 15th century and went on for a long time. In the facade the originality of the architectonic solution proposed by the artist (don't consider the staircase, which is a later addition) is already quite evident. Its classical elements - gable, arches, the light pilaster strips - give you a completely new impression.

In fact, they are elements reduced to the essential and the ornaments are almost inexistent, while a clean and slightly articulated surface dominates the whole.

The loggia situated on the right

side of the church, with its simple and harmonious architectonic lines, leads into the interior. This is Greek-cross shaped (having four arms of the same length) and strikes you with its simple and balanced structure. Notice the fine **tribune** and the **tombs** of some of the Belfiore Martyrs.

The **Crypt**, too, is an atmospheric and quiet place.

Following our route beyond May 24th Square, we reach Vittorio Veneto Square (where once the ancient Pusterla Gate was) and then, through the Tea Avenue, the Tea Palace.

THE TEA PALACE

It was built by order of Federico II Gonzaga, who wanted a quiet residence, where he could rest and enjoy himself in peace.

It is the architectonic masterpiece of Giulio Romano and one of the most interesting examples of an aristocratic house.

The original project referred to a much smaller "Villa", a sort of secondary residence.

But Giulio Romano himself, encouraged by the duke who was enthusiastic about Romano's project and wanted to exalt the magnificence of his court, designed it to be more complex and magnificent. And so, between 1525 and 1535, what was

The Tea Palace.

The Entrance of honour.

not a simple villa, but a true palace was built.

It is quadrangular, including a large interior courtyard as well.

We have said that this building may represent Giulio Romano's masterpiece.

As a matter of fact, if we compare it with his other works, we realize that the artist, though using the same architectonic canons and the usual classical elements, has given a new look to it, so much so that the effect of the whole is less evident, less radical and less scenographic. The surface, since it extends mainly in length, is quite balanced.

Rustication is not much in evidence and the whole architectonic structure seems more linear as it lies in the middle of the green surrounding it.

Thus we are faced with a different syntax, whose value is increased and exalted, thanks to the setting of the palace itself in the middle of nature with which it creates a new and positive symbiosis.

The interior, too, is to be attributed mainly to Giulio Romano, as far as the room-planning and the decorations are concerned.

The visit includes many halls, apart from the Garden and the Lodge of the Grotto adjoining the palace.

So we find in the following order:- the **Courtyard**, sumptuous and solemn;- the **Hall of the Sun**, so called for the subject represented on the vault, by Giulio Romano;- the **Metamorphoses Hall**, with frescoes representing themes from the Metamorphoses of Ovid;- the **Horse Hall**, with a wonderful wooden ceiling and the pictoral representation of the favourite horses of duke Francesco II,- the

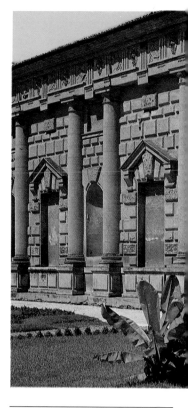

One of the monumental wings of the building.
Hall of the Horses.

Hall of Psyche, the most renowned hall of this palace, thanks to the beautiful frescoes covering its walls amost completely.

They were executed by Giulio Romano, with the help of various pupils.

Perhaps the artist has expressed here the best of his painting art. In various scenes he has represented the fine fable of Eros and Psyche, certainly hinting, under the discreet veils of a myth, at a probable love-story of the duke himself, and at the soul capable of freeing itself from various earthly tempta-

tions. Though they recall classical forms inspiring the figures of these frescoes, which are at the base of the narrative structure, and adhere to the canons of Raphael's art, these paintings stand out for their measured harmony of composition, immediate inspiration and lively scenes usually set in open and luminous landscapes.

The ornamental elements themselves characterizing the paintings of Giulio Romano, here are used with greater discretion and are better set into the narrative structure.

You should also notice the sagacity with which the artist has painted the plates and vases, thowing on them a solar light which embellishes them;- the **Zodiac Hall**, with the representation of the months and the signs of the Zodiac, all set into a strictly geometrical net-work; the **Eagles Hall**, where the beautiful ceiling is decorated with the representation of Phaeton falling from his cart.

Then we find the Tea Lodge, separating this first section of the Palace from the successive rooms.

In this second wing we find:- the **Stuccoes Hall**, so called because of the elegant stucco work adorning its walls and designing a long frieze on them. Primaticcio and Scutori worked on it;- **Caesar's Hall**: Giulio Romano, helped by some pupils of his, worked at this representation of Caesar's enterprises;- the **Giants' Hall**: with the magnificent frescoes of this room, the artist celebrated the victory of the emperor Charles V.

The subjects are drawn from designs by Giulio Romano, but they were executed by Rinaldo Mantovano. They represent the

The Hall of Psyche.

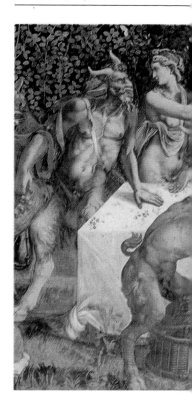

Giants falling from Olympus, after they rebelled against their king and were struck by lightning.

The scenes are apocalyptic, the magnificent figures dominate the room, while the scene of the stones, columns and giants falling down is very impressive. The tragedy, however, remains something purely exterior. - Some other rooms, smaller but decorated;- the **Octagons Hall**, with stucco decorated walls.

The visit to the Tea Palace ends with the **Garden** and the **Lodge of the Grotto**.

The latter is a small building, a little separated from the rest, but adjoining the main building. It shows fine and suggestive architecture, thanks also to its reduced dimensions.

The rooms of this house, too, not all perfectly kept, are decorated with frescoes or stuccoes, on which many artists worked.

The Zodiac Hall.

The Giants' Hall.

6th Route:

South-East Section - From the Belfiore Martyrs Square to Santa Maria of Gradaro and Cesare Gate Square.

Taking again the Belfiore Martyrs Square as a reference point, and taking September XX Street and then Frattini Street, we first come to an interesting **building** adorned with terracotta statues by Mantegna, the 17th century **Valenti Palace** and the Church of St. Egidius, dating back to the 18th century.

Having taken Garibaldi Avenue, we walk southward till the Thousand Square and then turn to the left, taking Gradaro Street and reach the **Church of Holy Mary of Gradaro**.

It is a beautiful and interesting building dating back to the latter half of the 13th century.

In the facade we notice that mixture of styles which characterized that period. Together with Romanesque elements, which had long been established, we notice Gothic elements, which had begun to be known all over Italy.

Notice also the elegant marble portal creating, in regard to the massive facade, an evident but simple decorative disconnection.

The interior of the Church is quite simple and linear: the style is Gothic.

The roof has a truss covering. One can admire interesting remains of Byzantine-like frescoes.

At the end of Garibaldi Avenue is the Cerese Gate Square, where the Cerese Gate once stood (one of the five gates which once opened along the town walls), but which is no longer standing.

Parma Street, which starts from this square, leads out of the town of Mantua.

Having crossed the railway, one can walk towards the Virgilian Wood and then towards Pietole, a small village situated on the place of the ancient Andes, Virgil's birth-place, of which we shall speak later.

MANTUA: ITS ENVIRONS AND PROVINCE

We shall try to follow some main routes, which, starting from Mantua's outskirts, will allow us to visit its immediate environs and then places farther off. In fact, in its province, there are many small towns or villages, spread all over the area, which, thanks to their beauty and importance, are part and parcel of the historical and cultural life of Mantua. So it is important to visit them not only to know this whole area better, but also to carry on the subject we have dealt with up to now.

1st ROUTE: from Mantua towards Cremona.

Church of Holy Mary of the Angels - Curtatone - Le Grazie - Casatico - Marcaria - Bezzolo.

The Sanctuary of Our Lady of the Graces.

Leaving the town and going towards Cremona, we find, first of all, two important religious buildings. Just near Mantua is the **Church of Holy Mary of the Angels**: it was built at the beginning of the 15th century and has a simple but elegant interior in Gothic style, as does the whole building. A beautiful painting of Mantegna's School, is situated above the altar, enclosed in a beautiful tabernacle.

Then come to **Curtatone**, which, together with Montanara, is connected to episodes of the wars for the independence of Italy. It was here that one of the most famous battles of the first war of indipendence took place (1848). A little further on there is the small village of **Le Grazie**, where one can admire the **Church of Holy Mary of Graces**. As a matter of fact, it is a Sanctuary, because long since, the image of the "Madonna" kept here, has enjoyed the devotion of the faithful. It was built, in the typical

Lombard Gothic style, between the end of the 14th century and the beginning of the 15th century. The long portico preceding the facade was built later. The interior, simple and elegant in its architecture and mainly in the apse, presents a peculiar decoration: in many niches situated along the walls, there are statues of miraculously-healed people and devotees in various attitudes. In the Sanctuary one can also admire the mausoleum of **Baldassarre Castiglione** and some quite interesting paintings by Lorenzo Costa (present here with "*St. Laurence's Martyrdom*"), Bazzani, F. Bonsignori, apart from the already mentioned image of the "*Madonna of Graces*" by an un-known 15th century author.

Then there is **Casatico**, the birth-place of Baldassarre Castiglione. In the built-up area one can admire the beautiful **Castiglione Castle**, which was the aristocratic house of this noble family. It consists of an articulated series of buildings surrounded by walls and towers, like a real castle.

Proceeding further on towards Cremona, one comes to the villages of **Marcaria**, **San Martino Dell'Argine** and then **Bozzolo**, a characteristic and lovely place at the borders of the province of Mantua. It was the seat of the Gonzaga court and of a side branch of this family, as shown by the beautiful ducal palace.

The Sanctuary of Our Lady of the Graces - the interior

2nd ROUTE: From Mantua towards Brescia.
The Fountain Wood - Marmirolo - Goito.

Once out of Mantua, across the Mills Bridge, taking the road leading towards Brescia, we come to, on a detour, the **Fountain Wood**. It covers a large area, forming a green oasis of quiet. Once it was even larger, when, belonging to the Gonzaga, it was used as a hunting and amusement park. In the middle of the wood, in a large bare patch called Prato (meadow), one can still admire the Gonzaga Cottage, one of the most beautiful buildings by Antonio Maria Viani, which looks rather like a castle. Then we go beyond **Marmirolo** towards Goito, having gone beyond some beautiful villas, including **Villa Moschini**, situated in the middle of a magnificent park. A little after the Church of our Lady of Health (18th century), we meet **Goito**, a town famous for the battle which took place here during the Italian Risorgimento. It is the birth-place of the Provençal poet Sordello.

The fountain Wood.

Among the places which can be easily reached from Mantua, we advise you to visit the **Favorita**.

We should say rather the ruins of the Favorita, since this is what remains of the luxurious and imposing out-of-town residence of the Gonzaga family. It dates back to the first decades of the 17th century. It was projected by the architect Nicolò Sebregondi in late-Renaissance style, under the patronage of Ferdinando Gonzaga.

From what today remains of that building (only a small part), one can imagine how imposing its architectonic structure must have been, so that it was more like a wonderful royal palace than a country residence.

Proceeding a little further (a few kilometres) one reaches the area of **Porto Mantovano** (so called because it was the port of Mantua) and **Corte Spinosa**, where we find an interesting group of buildings, which once belonged to the Gonzaga, surrounded by the houses and storehouses, where their servants lived and worked. They were projected and built by Giulio Romano.

Then comes **Roverbella**.

The Favorita

Coming out of the town across St. George's Bridge, one passes near a building known as **Sparafucile's house** (a character from the opera "Il Rigoletto" by Giuseppe Verdi). As a matter of fact, it was a defensive position of St. George's Castle.

Then one takes the road towards Legnago, passing near some villages and reaches **Castel D'Ario**, a village once belonging to Mantua's territory.

The remains of the castle are very beautiful and still impos-ing. The road leads to **Villimpenta**. This area, too, belonged to the Gonzaga, but previously it had belonged to the Scaligeri of Verona.

The **castle**, which is reflected with its towers and walls in the river Tione, still preserves intact its aspect as a powerful defensive stronghold. Near it there is the beautiful **Villa Zani**, built in Renaissance style for the Gonzaga family.

Villimpenta - the castle.

We come to various villages, some quite important, among the road leading from Mantua to Ferrara. Having passed **Governolo**, where, according to a tradition, Attila met Leo the Great, but more famous for historical events which took place here, one reaches **Ostiglia** a small town of Roman origin and today quite an important industrial centre.

Having crossed the Po, one reaches **Revere**. This territory, too, once belonged to the Gonzaga. One can visit the ducal palace built in the 15th century by Luca Fancelli, by order of duke Ludovico II Gonzaga. Still proceeding southward one comes to **Poggio Rusco**, whose Town Hall was one of the Gonzaga's residences, built by Luca Fancelli in the 15th century.

Revere - The Ducal Palace.

Leaving Mantua by Cerese Gate, one crosses first the **Virgilian Wood** and reaches **Pietole**, once Andes, the birthplace of the Latin poet Virgil, to whom a monument is dedicated. Having crossed the Po, one reaches **San Benedetto Po**, a fairly developed and economically active centre, mainly known for the famous **Abbey of St. Benedict**.

This building, dating back to the 10th-11th century, when it housed a community of Benedictine monks, must have gone through various historical events. The Abbey of Politone (as it is also called) developed in an area naturally defended by the rivers Po and Lirone (hence its name).

The church, becoming more and more important under the patronage of the Canossa family (countess Mathilda wanted to be buried here), also grew in size.

The main building, which at the beginning was only a chapel, was enlarged gradually according to the various tendencies of

The Basilica of St. Benedict - the Cloister.

87

art, such as the Romanesque, Gothic and Renaissance styles. The architect Giulio Romano, too, worked here, mainly as far as the re-structuring works were concerned. In the 17th century, too, renewal and enlargement works were executed. The magnificent Benedictine Abbey, renowned all over Italy, had changed its original look, but it had grown rich in important works from the historical and artistic point of view.

When, around the end of the 18th century, the religious order was suppressed, not only did all the works end, but the whole building declined.

Its main elements are the Basilica, the cloisters of St. Simeon, St. Benedict, the Abbots, and the sacristy.

The **Basilica**: in the facade and mainly in the lower part where the architecture is classical and quite simple, one can recognize the hand of Giulio Romano. The upper part was built later. The interior preserves, in its structure, the lines of Gothic art, while the decoration dates back to successive periods.

Various paintings and statues (by A. Begarelli) adorn its naves.

Of the three cloisters situated behind the Basilica (of St. Benedict, St. Simeon, the Abbots) the first one is the oldest, though it shows traces of the re-arrangements which took place in successive periods. That of the Abbots shows influences mainly by 17th century art, while that of St. Simeon has a beautiful portico with large Gothic arches. The **Sacristy**, built by Giorgio Romano, is particularly interesting. Various religious objects, illuminated books and ornaments dating back to various ages, are kept in it.

Many pictorial and sculptural works once adorned this building, but they were used to adorn other buildings and museums, when the monastery declined.

Having left San Benedetto Po and going southward, one reaches the small town of **Gonzaga**, also belonging to the dukedom of Mantua. One can see the remains of their **castle**. Notice particularly the fine square with porticoes.

The Basilica of St. Benedict - the choir.

Lastly we follow the route taking us to the borders of the ancient dukedom of Mantua, where it borders on Emilia. It will make known to us another important centre of great historical and cultural value, namely Sabbioneta.

SABBIONETA

It has been in the past, as it still is today, a small but very beautiful artistic centre. Sabbioneta, though belonging to the dukedom of Mantua, was ruled by a side branch of the Gonzaga family. Under the patronage of Vespasiano Gonzaga, it was completely renewed and became a town of art.

Therefore a visit to this palace is very interesting and gives you the possibilty of becoming better acquainted with the historical and cultural events which took place in Mantua. Though its monuments and buildings are not perfectly kept (the Castle has disappeared), the structure of its parts remains substantially intact. It is a true fortified town closed in a well organized structure made up of walls and towers, including a well ordered net-work of streets and buildings, recalling the town-planning of ancient Rome. Sabbioneta is thus a defensive stronghold, at the same time, an aristocratic residence, a town-residence, as it has been called, a rational structure meant to be the symbol of a well organized and harmonious town. From this point of view, it reveals the strong personality of Vespasiano Gonzaga, who had precisely this in mind and wanted it to be realized in this way.

Two gates lead into the town: the Imperial Gate and Victory Gate. **Victory Gate** was built in 1560. Notice in it the chromatic contrast between the white marbles framing the arch and the warm tonalities of the brick surfaces. The **Imperial Gate** was built twenty years later. This gate, completely covered with marbles, has, in the lower part, three arches (the middle one is the largest) and is surmounted by a gable.

The ideal centre of the town is the ancient ducal square, today called **Garibaldi Square** and surrounded by various buildings: the **Parish Church** dating back to the 16th century. In the interior, with only one nave, one can admire the Chapel of the Blessed Sacrament, with an original and evocative open-work dome, built by Antonio Bibiena in the 18th century;- the **Ducal Palace**: the building, finished in the latter half of the 16th century, shows quite simple architecture. In the lower fillet of the facade there is a series of five arches, surrounded by slight rustication work. In the upper fillet, with five windows, the building ends with a protruding cornice.

In its interior there was once a cycle of interesting decorations, of which only a part remains. One can admire mainly those in the **Ancestors' Hall**, where, apart from the portraits of the ancestors of the Gonzaga family,

89

Roman personages, mythological scenes and some fine landscapes are represented. In the other halls, apart from some remains of frescoes, one can admire the fine wooden ceilings.

Behind the Ducal Palace is the **Church of the Crowned Virgin**. It was the duke's chapel and was built between 1586 and 1588. Quite bare on the outside, with a forepart with three arches, it rises upwards with a rather vertical movement. The brick surfaces, with very warm tonality, have simple double windows and, on the upper part, a portico covered by a protruding penthouse. Such deep openings create a play of light and shade, which animate the whole building, without altering its structure. The octagonal interior shows a more striking and composite aspect, animated as it is by many chapels situated along the whole perimeter and by the overhanging portico. Here at his own request, is the Tomb of Vespasiano Gonzaga, built by G. B. Della Porta at the end of the 16th century. The bronze statue of the duke was made by Leone Leoni.

From Garibaldi Square, taking Theatre Street, one reaches the **Olympic Theatre**. It shows an elegant and composite architectonic structure, one of Vincenzo Scamozzi's works. The interior is very interesting for the original solution adopted by the artist. A wooden semicircular flight of steps leans against the back wall and above it there is an elegant portico with columns, adorned, on the upper part, with 12 statues. This was the place reserved for the Gonzaga family during performances. The stage underwent radical transformations, which have altered its structure.

From the Theatre, through Vespasiano Street, we reach the **Garden Palace** and the **Great Corridor**. The Great Corridor (the Ancients Gallery is here and can be reached from the Garden Palace) draws our attention with its sophisticated monumentality and architectonic language. It was built at the end of the 16th century.

Then there is the Garden Palace, so called because of the garden adjoining it. This building was the villa of the Gonzaga, though it was set into the town-walls. The outside aspect is quite simple and bare, while the interior is very beautiful with its rich and fine decorations, bearing wit-

Sabbioneta - The Ancients Gallery.

ness to the Maecenatism of the Gonzaga. This villa was also connected to the Castle (which has completely disappeared) and was the true residence of the Gonzaga. Its many rooms shows various decorations and pictoral representations. We shall mention here only some of them:- the **Room of Venus** - the **Room of the Graces** both with vaults with grotesque paintings by Fornaretto;- The **Mirrors Hall**, painted by Bernardino Campi with scenes representing *"sailing"*, *"hunting"*, *"walking"*, *"life in the fields"*, etc. , in which the artist creates delicate and pleasant effects.

- **Aeneas's Hall**, with lovely depictions drawn from episodes of Virgil's Aeneid.

- the **Ancients Gallery**: it is a very long hall (it occupies the interior of the Great Corridor), covered by a beautiful ceiling. It walls are completely frescoed. It was here that Vespasiano Gonzaga kept his collections of statues and various archeological pieces.

INFORMATION OFFICE
ATP. Piazza Mantegna 6, Tel. 328253 / Fax 363292

TRAVEL AGENCIES

AGENZIA VIAGGI COSMIK TOUR
Corso V. Emanuele, 9 / 11 — tel. 368847

AGENZIA VIAGGI LOTUS
Corso V. Emanuele, 17 — tel. 351171

AGENZIA VIAGGI PARTYTOUR
Corso V. Emanuele, 17 — tel. 322393

AGENZIA VIAGGI OK TRAVEL
Via Nievo, 13 — tel. 221111

AGENZIA VIAGGI UNITOUR
Via Verdi, 61 — tel. 363844

AGENZIA VIAGGI PASSEPARTOUR
P. zza 80⁻ Fanteria, 14 — tel. 360566

AGENZIA VIAGGI BETTINI
Piazza delle Erbe, 10 — tel. 368772

AGENZIA VIAGGI ARABESQUE
Via Trieste, 21 — tel. 366803

AGENZIA VIAGGI FACCHINI
Via Chiassi, 119 — tel. 222955

AGENZIA VIAGGI BARALDI TECNOTOUR
Via Campi, 9 — tel. 223222

AGENZIA VIAGGI GIRAMONDO
Via Calvi, 59 — tel. 350407

**ASSOCIAZIONE GUIDE TURISTICHE
ED INTERPRETI CASA DI RIGOLETTO**
Piazza Sordello, 23 — tel. 368917 - fax 223500

ORGANIZATIONS FOR SOCIAL AND YOUTH TOURISM

ASSOCIAZIONE CAMPEGGIATORI:
46047 S. Antonio P. M. (MN);
C. C. Mantova, c / o Ziviani, Via Volta, 16 — tel. 0376 / 397583
A. C. L. I. : Via Solferino, 36 — tel. 32718
Arci Nova: Str. Dosso del Corso, 2 / B
Com. Prov. — tel. 262555-6 / Fax 262565
ASS. GUIDE TURISTICHE
Città di Mantova: — tel 0330 / 716116

OTHER ORGANIZATIONS

ITALIA NOSTRA: c / o Geom. F. Orecchia,
Via Chiassi, 25 — tel. 325258
C. A. I. Sottoportico Lattonai, — tel. 328728
C. O. N. I. Via P. Amedeo, 29 — tel. 224454
SCI CLUB Via Arrivabene, 14 — tel. 362796

BOOK SHOPS

LIBRERIE DI PELLEGRINI(T. C. I.)
Corso Umberto I, — tel. 320333
LIBRERIA LUXEMBURG (T. C. I.)
Via Calvi, 27 — tel. 368169
LIBRERIA NAUTILUS (T. C. I.)
Piazza 80° Fanteria, 19 — tel. 323406

ADDRESSES OF GENERAL INTEREST

COMUNE DI MANTOVA : Via Roma, 39 — tel. 3381
BIBLIOTECA COMUNALE : Via Ardigò, 13 — tel. 338246
ARCHIVIO DI STATO : Via Ardigò, 11 — tel. 351243
AMMINISTRAZIONE PROVINCIALE
Via P. Amedeo, 30 — tel. 2041

QUESTURA: Piazza Sordello, 46 — tel. 2051

ADDRESSES OF GENERAL UTILITY

POLIZIA STRADALE:
Piazza Virgiliana, 27 — tel. 321707
CARABINIERI: Via Chiassi, 29 — tel. 328888
PRONTO INTERVENTO: — tel. 112
VIGILI DEL FUOCO:
Viale Risorgimento, 16 — tel. 221222
POLIZIA MUNICIPALE:
Viale Fiume 21 (angolo P. le Michelangelo) — tel. 320255

HEALTH SERVICES

OSPEDALE CIVILE «C. POMA»:
Via Albertoni, 1 — tel. 201413
PRONTO SOCCORSO:
Ambulanze — tel. 201201-201220
SERVIZIO VETERINARIO:
Piazza 80° Fanteria, 13 — tel. 201801
TOURISTIC ASSOCIATIONS:
(Uffici turistici della Provincia)

Acquanegra	tel. 0376 / 79101
ASOLA	tel. 0376 / 710070
BORGOFRANCO S / PO	tel. 0376 / 41622
CANNETO S / OGLIO	70131
CASTATICO (MARCARIA)	tel. 0376 / 95645
CASTELBERFORTE	tel. 0376 / 42158
Castelgoffredo	tel. 0376 / 7771
CASTEL D'ARIO	tel. 0376 / 660101
CASTELLUCCHIO	tel. 0376 / 438430
CASTIGLIONE D / STIVIERE	tel. 0376 / 632354
CAVRIANA	tel. 0376 / 82086
CERASARA	tel. 0376 / 87001
COMMESSAGGIO	tel. 0376 / 98146
CURTATONE (SEDE GRAZIE)	tel. 0376 / 31081
FELONICA	tel. 0376 / 66180
GAZZUOLO	tel. 0376 / 97117
GOITO	tel. 0376 / 60252
GOVERNOLO	tel. 0376 / 668423
MAGNACAVALLO	tel. 0376 / 55304
MARIA MANTOVANA	tel. 0376 / 735005
MEDOLE	tel. 0376 / 86001
MONZAMBANO	tel. 0376 / 80015
OSTIGLIA	tel. 0376 / 32225
POGGIO RUSCO	tel. 0376 / 733801
PIETOLE (VIRGILIO)	tel. 0376 / 440439
PIEVE DI CORIANO	tel. 0376 / 39131
QUISTELLO	tel. 0376 / 619729
REVERE	tel. 0376 / 46001
RIVALTA S / MINCIO (RODIGO)	tel. 0376 / 650777
RIVAROLO MANTOVANO	tel. 0376 / 99149
RONCOFERRATO	tel. 0376 / 663571
SABBIONETA	tel. 0376 / 52039
S. BENEDETTO PO	tel. 0376 / 615378
S. GIOVANNI DOSSO	tel. 0376 / 757314
SCHIVENOGLIA	tel. 0376 / 58277
SOLFERINO	tel. 0376 / 854068
SUSTINENTE	tel. 0376 / 43373
VIADANA	tel. 0376 / 81006
VILLA POMA	tel. 0376 / 565131
VOLTA MANTOVANA	tel. 0376 / 83116

Art galleries, museums, picture galleries, historical villas of artistic interest.

MANTUA

PALAZZO DUCALE: Piazza Sordello, tel. 0736 / 320283-320586.Tue - Sat: 9. 00-13. 00 / 14. 30-16. 30 Sundays and holidays: 9. 00-13. 00. Mon: 14. 30-16. 30.

PALAZZO TE: Viale Te tel. 0376 / 323266-365886 Mon - Sun: 13.00-18. 00. Tickets until 17.30 closed on 1.1 - 1.5 - 25.12.

PALAZZO D'ARCO: Piazza D'Arco 1- tel. 1376 / 323342,NOVEMBER / FEBRUARY Sundays and Holidays: 9. 00-12. 00 / 14. 30-16. 00. MARCH / OCTOBER: Tue - Wen - Fry: 9. 00-12. 00. Thu - Sat - Sun - holidays: 9. 00-12. 00 / 15. 00-17. 00. Mon closed.

MUSEO F. GONZAGA: Piazza Virgiliana 55, tel. 0376 / 320602-322051 (Curia) NOVEMBER / MARCH - Sun - only 9. 30-12. 00 / 14. 30-17. 00 - APRIL / JUNE 9. 30-12. 00 / 14. 30-17. 00 - Mon closed. JULY / AUGUST Thu-Sat- Sun: 9. 30-12. 00 / 14. 30 - 17. 00. SEPTEMBER / OCTOBER: 9. 30-12. 00 / 14. 30-17.00 - Mon closed.

MUSEO DEL RISORGIMENTO: Piazza Sordello 42 Open on request c/o P. Ducale, tel. 0376 / 320283.

TEATRO ACCADEMICO BIBIENA: Viale Accademia 47 tel. 1376 / 327653: 9. 00-12. 30 / 15. 00-17. 30, Sun closed.

MUSEO TAZIO NUVOLARI: Piazza Broletto 9 ,tel. 0376 / 327929: 9. 00-13. 00 / 15. 00-18. 00. Mon and thu morning closed.

CASA DEL MANTEGNA: Viale Acerbi 47 tel. 1376 / 360506-326685: 8. 00 / 12. 30 / 15.00- 18.00. Free entrance.

THE PROVINCE

ASOLA
Museo Civico Archeologico "G. Bellini"
Viale Brescia 8 - tel. 0376 / 710542, Sun and holidays: (winter) 10. 00 - 12.·00 / 14. 00-17. 00. (Summer) 10. 00-12. 00 / 15. 00-18. 00.

CASTIGLIONE DELLE STIVIERE
Museo Internazionale Croce Rossa
Via Garibaldi 50 tel. 0376 / 638505
October - March: 9. 00-12. 00 / 14. 00-17. 30
April - September: 9. 00-12. 20 / 15. 00-19. 00
Mon closed.

Museo Storico Aloisiano
Via Perati 8 tel. 0376 / 638062-639590
October - May: 9. 00-11. 00 / 15. 00-17. 00
June - September: 9. 00-11. 00 / 15. 00-18. 00

CAVRIANA
Museo Archeologico dell'Alto Mantovano
Piazza Castello 5 tel. 0376 / 82094
November - February: Sun 15. 00-18. 00 - March - October: Thu. Sat. Sun. 9. 00-12. 00 / 15. 00-18. 00 - Mon closed.

GAZOLDO DEGLI IPPOLITI
Museo d'arte moderna dell'Alto Mantovano
Via Marconi - tel. 0376 / 657141
Tue - Sun: 9. 00-12. 00 / 14. 30-18. 30
Mon closed. Free entrance.

SOLFERINO - Cappella Ossario - Museo La Roc-

ca - Memoriale Croce Rossa Italiana
tel. 0376 / 854068
January: Sat and Sun 9. 00 - 12. 00 / 14. 00-17. 00 - February / November / December (Mon closed): 9. 00-12. 00 / 14. 00-17. 00
March / October(Mon closed): 9. 00-12. 30 / 14. 00-18. 00 - April - September:(closed Mon): 9. 00-12. 30 / 14. 30-18. 30 - closed from 16 to 31 December.

SUZZARA - Galleria Civica d'Arte Contemporanea
Via G. Rossa 48 / B tel. 1376 / 535593
Summer :working days 16. 00-19. 00
Holidays 10. 00-12. 30 / 16. 00-19. 00
15. 00-18. 00 - free entrance - Mon closed.

VIADANA - Museo Archeologico "A. Parazzi"
Via Verdi - tel. 1375 / 830747,Tue, Fri, Sun: 9. 00-12. 00. Free entrance.

MAIN CULTURAL EVENTS IN THE YEAR

FEBRUARY / CASTEL GOFFREDO
"Carnevale" With the traditional crowning of the "Re Gnocco"
FEBRUARY / CASTEL D'ARIO
Traditional Carnival with «La Bigolada»
APRIL / OSTEGLIA
Spring Fair
(exhibitions, meetings, artistic events, contests, concerts; etc.)
APRIL-MAY / SABBIONETA
National antique-trade fair
MAY / VILLIMPENTA
Risotto festival
MAY / MANTUA
Yearly fair of books and ancient prints
JUNE / VIADANA
S. Pietro fair. Melon, ham and lambrusco festival
JULY / POGGIO RUSCO
Yearly fair «Basso Po» mantovano
JULY / RIVALTA s / MINCIO
Mincio river festival
JULY / REVERE
Traditional fair(Po festival)
AUGUST / S. BENEDETTO PO
Traditional August fair
AUGUST / GRAZIE
August holiday festival: yearly meeting with the «Madonnari»
SEPTEMBER / GONZAGA
«Millenaria» fair (agricultural show, stands, exhibitions, etc.)
SEPTEMBER / GONZAGA
A. R. I. fair
SEPTEMBER / RIVALTA s / MINCIO
Hunting, fishing and sport implements fair
SEPTEMBER / MONZAMBANO
Grape-festival and country gastronomy
OCTOBER / S. BENEDETTO PO
"Nedar festival" (folk and cultural shows)
OCTOBER / CANNETO s / OGLIO
Biennial fair of toys and nursery plants
NOVEMBER / MANTUA
Teatro Sociale. Opera season.

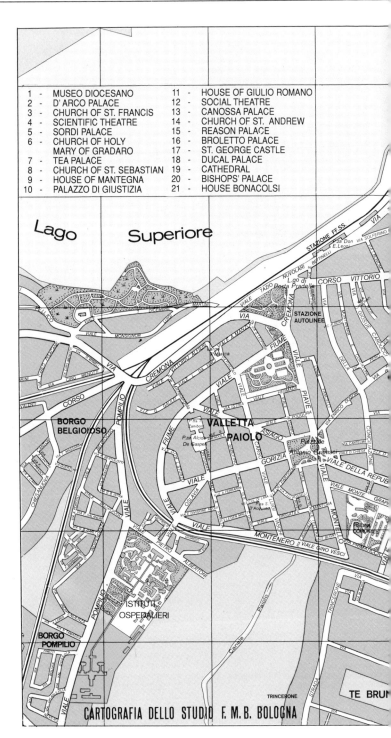

1 -	MUSEO DIOCESANO	11 - HOUSE OF GIULIO ROMANO
2 -	D' ARCO PALACE	12 - SOCIAL THEATRE
3 -	CHURCH OF ST. FRANCIS	13 - CANOSSA PALACE
4 -	SCIENTIFIC THEATRE	14 - CHURCH OF ST. ANDREW
5 -	SORDI PALACE	15 - REASON PALACE
6 -	CHURCH OF HOLY	16 - BROLETTO PALACE
	MARY OF GRADARO	17 - ST. GEORGE CASTLE
7 -	TEA PALACE	18 - DUCAL PALACE
8 -	CHURCH OF ST. SEBASTIAN	19 - CATHEDRAL
9 -	HOUSE OF MANTEGNA	20 - BISHOPS' PALACE
10 -	PALAZZO DI GIUSTIZIA	21 - HOUSE BONACOLSI

CARTOGRAFIA DELLO STUDIO F. M. B. BOLOGNA

INDEX

Photographs: Archive Plurigraf
APT Mantova - Toni Lodigiani page 70 - 71.

© Copyright by Casa Editrice Plurigraf
S. S. Flaminia, km 90 - 05035 Narni - Terni - Italia
Tel. 0744 / 715946 - Fax 0744 / 722540 - (Italy country code: +39)
All rigts reserved. No Part of this publication may be reproduced.
Printed: 1996 - Plurigraf S. p. A. - Narni

L. 7.000
I.V.A. INCLUSA